AF421978

PAPA, DOES THE RAILROAD TRACK GO ALL THE WAY TO WHERE THE SUN GOES DOWN?

By

Sandy Black

515 South Flower Street, 18th and 19th Floors,
Los Angeles, California, 90071

ISBN: 978-1-83663-035-7

Library of Congress Number: 2022915634

You may visit her at her website: booksbysandyllc.com
and email: blackbrunson5@gmail.com

This book is a work of fiction. Names, characters, places are a
product of the authors imagination.

Table Of Contents

Acknowledgements

In memory of several friends lost this year. Each supported and contributed to all of the "Fun Books by Sandy" books I have written.

They will be missed.

A special thanks to Madison, Indiana and all who supported my research efforts. And a special shout out to those who helped give life and wings to the future books I write.

Chapter One
Don't Go Near That Railroad Depot Today — Hear? We Won't Mama

Irvie, Tyrone, Mel, Stymie and Gar are so excited they could hardly sleep a wink. Fully dressed, shoes beside their beds, little brown lunch sacks on the back porch modestly filled with jam and peanut butter sandwiches, and a freshly picked Red Haven peach — compliments of Tyrone. His mama's basket sits ready for the days canning event. Now minus five peaches.

It was suggested by Gar that there would be little time for runnin' home for lunch. Seemingly, the 'band of 5' had thought out every detail for the biggest awaited secret excursion of the year.

Like every other late summer day, regardless of the humidity that you could cut with a knife, the 'spirited 5' gathered at Irvie's playground. A broken piece of fence easily slipped through near the old Rosen Farm that provided at least an acre for playing hide and seek, bicycle antics, pond fishing and creek dipping which required swinging on the rope over the creek. Just to see how far you could go out for champion belly flop bragging rights. Most important was always to plot that next summer days events.

Today Is Special - Really Special

"What's all the ruckus about?" ask 'Kitty Sydnoi', the trusted bodyguard and resident cat at The Anna Depot. "I'm a bit busy here can't you see?" grumpily bellowed The Ann Depot. "My telegraph is making a lot of racket today. Makes my head ache from the rattling of windows."

'Kitty Sydnoi' ran out. "Okay! Okay! I'm going out to lay on the bench and wait on the New York Central #3 comin' in soon. It's going to pull off on the spur for the 3 o'clock connection to Indianapolis and I heard there was a special delivery comin' off the train today."

'Kitty Sydnoi' watched for the usual rowdy "locals," well knowing each of their mama had admonished them not to go play near the railroad or The Anna Depot today. "Here they come. I knew it. No time for nappin' now," said 'Kitty Sydnoi'.

The Anna Depot said, "Shh! be still. Mr. Horace Jeffers, our telegraph operator got a big and important message. He is peckin' on that little thing that tells him stuff and sends messages down to the next Depot. Today we were just told the delivery of the new movie house glass screen is expected to be on the 1:10, and that's exciting news."

"Be still Tyrone. You, too, Mel or I'm gonna 'box your ears' just like your mama's gonna do if she catches us here," said Irvie. "The train be comin' soon." "You know what?" said Gar. "If we go on the other side of The Anna Depot's porch, we can crawl underneath and see the big glass screen when they unload it off the train. Then we can run down behind the flat bed truck and beat it to the movie house. Whata you guys think?" "Yeah, we could run around to the back cellar door. Nobody will know we are down there," said Stymie.

"But dog gone it, you guys gotta be quiet. If anyone sees us, we are gonna be in big trouble," said Irvie, who seemed to be in charge.

'Kitty Sydnoi' observing all the mischievous planning, quickly ran ahead and under The Anna Depot porch. "One, two, three, run!" Tyrone leading the pack with Mel pulling up the rear. Each getting through the slatted board of the old, weathered porch and took a perfect viewing position. The New York Central #3 was usually right on time at 1:10.

'Kitty Sydnoi' quietly whispered to The Anna Depot,

"I'll just stay down here with the secret guests — you know, kind of watch for New York Central #3's Conductor, Haddad. He doesn't have much of a sense of humor for the kids hanging around the train just having summer fun. They might need warned for a quick getaway." The Anna Depot just laughed. "His bark is bigger than his bite, but he'll sure try to scare the dickens out of 'em."

"What?! A fire? On the train? Which car?" Mr. Horace Jeffers, the Telegraph Operator came running out of The Anna Depot. "Help! Help! Car #4 is on fire. Get the hoses. Hurry. Do something! A spark from the wheels on the spur line ignited the grass and started a big fire." "I told Henry he should keep those weeds cleaned out of the path of the tracks," said The Anna Depot. The train is crawling to the water tower. Brakemen Dean and Bobbie Whitmeer are racing up the steps of the water tower. Their aim is to quickly lower the arm so water can flow all over car #4. It has been raining for several days off and on. The cooler weather has made the water very cold.

All of a sudden, people began to scream and scatter. "Oh no! The glass is shattering," said 'Kitty Sydnoi'. The five 'invisible' boys did not move a muscle or say a word. 'Kitty Sydnoi' ran over and jumped on Irvie's lap. No one had ever seen anything like this before. The big glass screen began to fly in all directions. It was soon reduced to only shards and chunks of glass, and the train was a total disaster with glass and metal all over the track making it impossible to move.

The five shocked friends who were still huddled under The Anna Depot porch decided to crawl out and investigate. Seems they weren't the only kids in town who came down for the special delivery. Word travels fast in a small town in Ohio.

The bigger pieces of glass all over the ground were like finding a surprise birthday gift. "Look Tyrone, it's a magnifying glass," said Gar. "Don't tell anybody 'cause now we can see bugs and all sorts of stuff." "Irvie, do you have a bandage? asked Mel. I just cut my finger and I might bleed to death!" Irvie cackled out loud. "Don't be silly, it's only a scratch you dummy. You are looking at it through the magnifying glass." "C'mon guys, we gotta go pick up our pennies on the railroad track before someone else finds them. Gonna be no train to flatten them today!" "We better head home. I don't know about you, but I'm late for dinner." Stymie told his exhausted friends.

The Anna Depot, Telegraph Operator, Mr. Horace Jeffers, Conductor, Mr. Haddad and the Brakeman,

Whitmeer brothers spent the next few days with the train investigators hashing over the details of one of the biggest events to ever roll through town on the New York Central Railroad while Kitty Sydnoi continued a well-deserved nap.

It was suggested that a few of the town's summer rascals, who participated without permission, did not offer their birds eye view of the events observed from beneath The Anna Depot porch. Some may well had a lickin' waiting on them when they got home and not just for being late for dinner.

Kitty Sydnoi giggled and said, "Been pretty quiet down here. Thinkin' the bench outside The Anna Depot may just be empty awhile. Sorta void of train travelers and those who may be having a little trouble sitting down. "I'm thinkin' Irvie, Tyrone, Mel, Stymie, and Gar are gonna be real glad when school starts."

The Anna Depot agreed, "At least they will go off restriction and no doubt deliver the best "What I Did For Fun This Summer" paper ever read by Mrs. Barr in English 101.

Chapter Two
From Railroad Engineer to Railroad Telegraph Operator to a "Harvey Girl" ...Huh?

'Kitty Tiffin' lay quietly on the bench outside Depot #113 where Jenna Oxley practiced her big announcement speech to be given at tomorrow's family Saturday brunch.

"Father, I've decided to go to college and be either a railroad engineer or a railroad telegraph operator." "All through high school, Mr. McMurphy let me tidy Depot #113, watch him send dot, dot messages, sort tickets, and I know I would be good at it." "I made all A's in my chemistry and math classes." 'Kitty Tiffin' remarked to Depot #113, "She better wait until after brunch because her father will raise the roof, her mother will faint, and her grandmother will no doubt quote scriptures in the Bible that state every reason why women don't do certain things, if you know what I mean."

"Boy, am I glad I'm standing at the Elm and Main intersection," said #113 Depot. "Yup, you just watch, the windows will surely be rattling and you'll need a boat for

Mrs. Oxley's tears,." 'Kitty Tiffin' giggled under his beautiful, golden brown whiskers.

Usual Saturday morning. The house maid rang the bell and Jenna, along with her faithful 'Kitty Tiffin', went downstairs. After everyone seemed to have had their fill of brunch and Father had finished his newspaper with usual comments on current events, Jenna made her announcement.

As predicted Mr. Oxley, in a matter-of-fact voice said, "I don't know where that came from, but it's not happening. Most ridiculous thing I have ever heard. We won't discuss this again." Jenna's mother was much more animated. "Why, you are a baby, you have never been away from home, and your grandmother has already told Mrs. McWaters that you will watch her children this summer while she volunteers for the new Women's League. Now no more nonsense talk." Emma, clear the table please," Mrs. Oxley has spoken!

Mr. Oxley's morning paper fell off the sideboard, and 'Kitty Tiffin' raced out from beneath the table to see if any morsels of toast or cook Madaline's peach scones that may have fallen on the carpet. Jenna picked up the paper and a big wanted ad jumped out at her. A picture of a neatly dressed girl in a uniform standing beside a big locomotive in the background. It read:

WANTED

Young women. 18 to 30 years of age, of good character to work on the Santa Fe Railroad in the West at Harvey Eating Houses.

No experience needed. Good wages with room and meals furnished.

Apply: The Fred Harvey Company.

"'Kitty Tiffin', I am going to apply. You know. I could be a Harvey Girl! I remember the Santa Fe Railroad all the way from Chicago to California when I worked with Mr. McMurphy at the Depot."

"Oh dear, thought 'Kitty Tiffin', we get to hear a new announcement and Grandma Oxley will be there. Now that is gonna be scary."

Days went by and many sleepless nights for Jenna. Also, hours spent hovering over the mailbox waiting on a response from The Fred Harvey Company. Then **IT** came. 'Kitty Tiffin' crawled upon Jenna's lap just in case there was bad news.

Jenna carefully opened the long, elegant looking

envelope. Her heart was beating a mile a minute. All of a sudden, Jenna grabbed 'Kitty Tiffin' and nearly squeezed the life out of her. "I got an interview! I got an interview! But it has to be a secret!!"

The day finally came. 'Kitty Tiffin' sat in the Depot #113 waiting patiently for Jenna to return from the big interview. While waiting, The Depot #113 said, "I'm a bit worried. Some people say the Harvey Girls are nothing more than ... 'Kitty Tiffin' firmly interrupted, "That is just ignorant rumor mill talk and idle gossip. I know for a fact that all those ladies are selected because they are 'real' ladies, are of high moral fiber and come from reputable families. 'Kitty Tiffin' said "I don't think that "houses of ill-repute" has any truth to it." "You are probably right," said Depot #113. "I won't breathe another word."

The Decision Announcement

Saturday morning brunch again. "I'm going to be a Harvey Girl! I went on an interview and got hired and I leave for Emporia, Kansas on Thursday."

Mother grabbed her neatly starched napkin, covered her mouth, and told the kitchen maid to leave the room. "You are ruined, might as well be a saloon girl." Grandmother Oxley let out a gasp. "Why she will never get a marriage proposal now! And where is Emporia anyway? We will be the laughing stock of the town. Marjorie Hanover's daughter is engaged to Banker Waywards' son, who is going to be an accountant. Why she will be President of the Homemakers Guild in no time. And you …Oh! I'm going to bed. I think I'm going to need a doctor."

The Next Day

"'Kitty Tiffin', I am so excited. I have gone over every line of the list a hundred times."

-No loud talking in rooms

-10:00 PM curfew

-Clean bathtubs after use

-No chewing gum

-Hair must be pulled back

-Black stockings and black shoes only

-Wear only Harvey provided (4) uniforms. one to wear, one in laundry and two spare

-Skirt 8" from floor. And that means 8"

- Starch and iron white apron

"'Kitty Tiffin', I want to be the best drink girl ever. Not sure I will ever learn The Cup Code." She smiled down at her friend who was already nodding off after another long day.

Later, 'Kitty Tiffin' chatted with Depot #113 about the silly cup thing. Depot #113 said, "What difference does it make if you order coffee and the cup sits upside down or if tea handles have to sit a certain way." "Really 'Kitty Tiffin'?" "I know," said 'Kitty Tiffin', but remember, "It's The Harvey Way."

Six Months Later

After polishing, and more polishing, wearing an apron so stiff it could stand up by itself, no sitting down even during long shifts, following lists and rules to the letter, all original six girls were individually called into Miss McPhearson's room and told if they had passed or failed the Harvey School of Hospitality. Jenna thought, "I may be going home."

"Jenna Oxley, I am pleased to tell you that you are now a "Harvey Girl." You received high marks in all sections, and you will be going on the Atchison, Topeka &

Santa Fe Railroad to the newest Harvey House in Belin, New Mexico. "Congratulations and welcome aboard!"

That night, Jenna wrote home:

Dear Father and Mother,

I'm now on my way to Belin, New Mexico. I have passed all my Harvey House Hospitality classes and am an official Harvey Girl and makes $50 a month. I have learned so much about railroad crews, the conductors, engineers, brakemen, flagmen, and even engine wipers—a job I don't desire to hold. The next time you see me, I will not be a "Harvey Girl." I have enrolled in the New Mexico School of Railroad Engineering. Who knows, maybe you will see me on the Atchison, Topeka & Santa Fe. We make one stop at Depot #113 as we pass through to Chicago.

Your loving daughter,

Jenna and 'Kitty Tiffin'

Chapter Three
Might Not Wanna Mess with the
Wrecking Boss's Wife

'Kitty Kiddly' yawned and stretched. Not unusual to be awakened in the night because Mr. Hutcheson got a call.

One might say being married to a railroad wrecking engineer is similar to a doctor's wife. Both have long hours away from home and constant emergencies requiring them to be on call 24/7.

'Kitty Kiddly' curled up near the fireplace while Mr. Hutcheson, her master, refreshed his shaving kit, and packed several shirts and socks. This newest railroad derailment sounded bad and no doubt would take several weeks to get the crippled locomotive back to a location where it could be repaired.

Bill Hutcheson loved his work and his new wife. However, recently promoted to Wrecking Foreman, and being moved to the Kansas prairie with its flatland and few trees made cleaning up a train wreck more difficult.

'Kitty Kiddly', the family Persian cat and Karin

Hutcheson woke up with a normal Kansas day in mind. However, the day would be anything but ordinary. On the table sat a newly packed, but forgotten, kester, the small grip filled with all Mr. Hutcheson's two weeks shaving and clothing needs.

"Come on, 'Kitty Kiddly'. We have to catch the next train. Wives of wrecking engineers rate a pass, so we will just take the next train and hand deliver Bills' kester."

'Kittiy Kiddly' saw this as an opportunity. He gave a big Persian shout out! "We are Ottawa bound. This means I get to meet up with my old friends inside the cooks' car. We'll be just in time for breakfast." Since Karin used to work as a waitress in Harvey dining rooms alongside the Santa Fe tracks, she knew a good home cooked meal by the smell. Those were the days before she married Mr. Hutcheson. 'Kitty Kiddly' was part of a litter born in the Harvey House. All Persian fur babies were adopted by Harvey girls.

Most pressing now was getting all the railroaders fed and out to the latest wreck. Numerous cars of crude oil and gasoline had broken loose and went flying downhill. As the train rounded the curve with full force, it hit the bridge. Five cars tumbled into the river.

What came next was miraculous. Men skillfully

worked the wrecking derrick. Perilous work trying to get the fire out from the burning oil which also melted overhead girders. No fatalities but several men were hurt as they crawled over the twisted steel of the wrecked bridge.

One of the reasons Karin was selected as a Harvey Girl was that she had gone to college two years and majored in Nursing. She called out to 'Kitty Kiddly', "Let's go girl. We need to find the med-kit/ first aid chest usually found in the cook car. These men are going to need tending to!" 'Kiddy Kiddly' began to make hissing sounds. The head engineer was shouting, "No train running outa Ottawa! Water has gone over the bridge. The depot made of logs has lost parts of its station platform. No water, lights, or telegraph. "How will we get home?" 'Kitty Kiddly' wondered.

Someone yelled, "We have a train going to the junction north of Ottawa. Karin told 'Kitty Kiddly' to jump in her valise because things there might be pretty bad. She was right. Chaos was everywhere. Fires, trees uprooted, debris floating and those that could slosh through the water to a bunk car. After helping several men exhausted but with only minor injuries, Karin said "I think we should crawl into a bunk for a few minutes. I'm cold and I know you are as well. We are exhausted and could use a short nap."

Both were sleeping soundly when linemen were heard bringing in some wounded men. The Lineman Foreman said, "You can't take them in there. The Wrecking Foreman's wife and cat are resting. Immediately, Karin Hutcheson popped her head up and said, "Oh, yes you can and will! Lay two in the lower bunk and two in the upper, and I will take care of them. I have some medical supplies and training. Now put more coal on the pot belly stove so I can boil some water. If you come back later, I will also have a pot of coffee brewing. Now get out of my infirmary! We have work to do!

'Kitty Kiddly' crawled out from the bunk covers, looked up with pride at her mistress and smiled.

Mr. Hutcheson will be so proud and "I just love trains."

Chapter Four
A Different Kind of Railroad — of the
Underground Kind

"Gotta hurry 'Kitty Rudley'. Get up in this ole' cotton sack," said the runaway slave, Odis Mosley. "They think we dumb, don't know nothin' but pickin' cotton. Slaves and cotton — cotton and slaves."

Mr. Odis said, "I hear Masta McAlister say he was gonna go buy a few darkies 'cause he has the biggest crop ever growed here and he need more slaves for pickin'. 'Kitty Rudley' jumped up on Mr. Odis' lap, stretched up tall and yelled, "'Kitty Klover', you best get over here now! We be leavin' soon to help Mr. Mosley and three other slave families start our journey. We are headin' to freedom."

Mr. Odis took his weathered and scarred hand and smoothed out the furry, matted, black coat of his faithful friend and traveling companion. This time, the travel will be life threatening for all — if caught.

"Masta gonna be mad, real mad when he find out we are gone when he get back," said 'Kitty Rudley'. "He just mean for sport," replied 'Kitty Klover' "Let's go!"

Mr. Odis Mosley gathered everyone together. Each family is willing to risk their lives by leaving Kentucky. We all will head North together to the Ohio River and beyond. Wherever freedom takes them.

Mr. Odis said to the other fugitive slaves, "What Masta don't know about us is that we have learned to read and write a bit. Enough to get us by. Masta gave me an awful beatin' once 'cause I slipped up and read a SLAVES FOR SALE sign out loud. That's when they took my Nella and two boys — sold 'em next day. We're gonna be free one day and I'm gonna find 'em.

With everyone in a tight circle under a sky that had clouds so big they covered the moon, and in the darkest of night, the escape plan was laid out all the way to Madison, Indiana. If all goes as planned, they soon would be crossing the Ohio River and then North to Canada. Mr. Odis thought it was a good thing that there was less moon shining down so brightly. It would make travel easier.

Mr. Odis quietly said, "We must first get ourselves, while Masta McAlister is gone to the 'darkie' sale to the Wentworth Lime Caves. It's gonna be awful wet, cold, nasty smellin' and real scary. But, no matter what, there can be no talkin' or stoppin' until we get to the first wall markings on the cave wall. Them cave tunnels, I'm told will be dark, but there are markings for us which will show where the houses stand that are built above the ground. The hidden doors are marked, and people called "Conductors" will be at designated places to help us. This is part of the new "Underground Railroad."

"Quaker families, and others including our black runaway friends, who have successfully escaped, will be there with food and warm blankets. After a brief rest, we will go on to the next cave house. The man at the third cave house will take us to the woods, and on to a church across the river. Now, enough talking— a lot of walking ahead of us and each of you knows your job!!"

"When we come out of the caves, we gotta move fast, 'Kitty Rudley' said to his friend 'Kitty Klover'. Our job is very important in the woods 'cause there may not be any Conductors to help us, and we could be on our own. Bounty hunters scare Conductors away sometimes. Also, we may be called upon to help more runaway slaves than just those in our group. If we get out, I'm told that not only will the caves smell ugly, but other things live in there!! 'Kitty Klover' said, "What kind of things?" Never mind. Right now, I'm thinkin' we need to just worry about what the woods will be like. Mr.

Odis says the trees are so tall that the tops whistle like 100 fans in church on a hot Sunday mornin'."

Mr. Odis now in a low whispering tone, continued sharing the next step in the escape plan. "The dark woods with brush thick and thorny can't be any worse than the caves I wouldn't think. Now this is what we will be looking for. Nails put in trees driven in a certain pattern, stakes in the road where the road forks and a sap holder turned sideways on a tree. You two Kitty's know at times the fog will be so thick you can't see one another and we will need you to slip through the trees unnoticed and stop at the fork."

'Kitty Rudley' said, "Sometimes slave hunters are sneaking around, so if we see or hear them, we make loud hawk-like noises. Mr. Odis, he knows my sound and what to do to keep from gettin' caught. We done practiced that!" Kitty Rudley continued to explain to his friend, "If we all make it through the caves, through the woods and across the Ohio River, there will be a flat, homemade barge hidden near the water. A Quaker family will be waiting with food and warm blankets. We will then be on the Indiana side of the Ohio River. Our final part of our journey will be in a false bottom wagon. We will be hidden under fruit and vegetables driven by farmers who help runaway slaves get into Madison and on North to freedom."

"Kitty Klover" asked, "Can we trust all these white folk?" Her friend replied, "Mr. Mosley told me we would be meeting a trusted friend, a member of the Neils Creek Anti-Slavery Society and we have been instructed to talk to no one else. He reminded us that the punishment for getting caught will be branding with a cow prod or even death. If caught, he would never live long enough to be reunited with his beloved Nella and his boys."

Mr. Odis Mosley, three other fugitive runaways, and his trusted companions successfully escaped thanks to the support of the people involved with the Underground Railroad. A railroad not made of steel rails, wooden ties, or trains, but a movement of people with a common vision. Blacks working with whites for one purpose. To help fugitive black families escape the bonds of slavery and live a free and productive life.

Mr. Odis Mosley became a dairy farmer. He, among many others, resisted slavery with their hearts and souls. Nella Mosley and one son were reunited with Odis Mosley.

Some say, 'Kitty Rudley' and 'Kitty Klover' can be found in the barn. No hiding in a cotton sack, but laying on fresh straw near Gussie, the cow. Of course, near all the milk they can drink.

Kitty Klover has a new litter to feed. All born free!!

Between 1810 and 1850, the Underground Railroad helped one hundred thousand enslaved people to freedom.

Chapter Five

Do Cabooses and Cats Have Nine Lives?

"Hey, for a caboose, you're a good-looking fella. Bright red and all." 'Kitty Jewel' remarked as the little red caboose slowed down. "I'm just grateful we did not have another wreck. 'Kitty Jewel', I am an old wooden caboose with a tiny bobber. I even have a cupola and am 22 ft. long. I have sure seen a lot in my day."

"You know, I bunk with the Chef. He fixes some pretty fine vittles for the construction crew right out of this little kitchen. Sometimes the brakemen who "tie down" the cars have to draw straws for the jump seats. Of course, there is always a little extra grub for you 'Kitty Jewel'.

'Kitty Jewel' has been watching and listening to the caboose who seems really worried these days. "With all the craziness and unknown changes around him, 'Kitty Jewe'l thought, "I'm thinking he should talk to the Eel River Railroad Depot about it. Together, they might come up with a solution or two."

'Kitty Jewel', you are teased a lot about your legendary nine lives, but now our railroad is being compared to you!" laughed the little red caboose.

The Eel River Railroad Depot said, "Like you, 'Kitty Jewel', we seem to land on our feet, and just carry on as though we have a few lives left to live."

The little caboose said, "We just have begun to realize our 'A Farm to Market' dream of having a better way to transport our crops and people could soon become a reality." "But all of a sudden now our caboose fleet, as well as many train depots, is going to have to make some big changes. I heard there are far too many rear-end collisions, and I may be replaced with all steel parts. Something called air brakes and automatic couplers. Whatever in the world that is. Not sure I want to find out."

'Kitty Jewel' said, "Seems we been having everything under the sun that could go wrong — go wrong times two. Why we had two depots hit by lightning this month! And don't forget 'The Church Street Wreck'. A water tower sprung a leak and froze. Yup, froze the track. What a mess! 13-50 freight train cars derailed. That sure brought things to a screachin' halt."

The ERR Depot said, "It would be so sad if our depot, which is the center for social happenings in town were to become a ghost town like the ones hit by lightning. Why, we would not have a need for our beautiful, old, mahogany-colored benches which are all lined up outside just waiting on those who might get off the train. People buying tickets, no chattering of the old brass telegraph key, or no more sounder with the Prince Albert tobacco can that reflects the sounds. There would be no people going or coming. Why isn't someone doing something about making our railroads, depots and trains (including cabooses) more safe?"

The little caboose looked at his friend and said, "Maybe, just maybe the changes will be good and our 'Farm to Market' dream will still become a reality. The little caboose, and 'Kitty Jewel' looked at each other and cracked up laughing. "How many lives did you say we have left?"

Chapter Six
Oh! The Summer of 1854 on The Orphan Train

"Charlie, shut up! You're gonna mess everything up. They told me I would get a new dress, and shoes 'n socks. Ain't never had a dress or shoes before. What's an Orphan Train anyway?"

Charlie looked down at his little sister, Meda, holding the only thing she owned and cherished, 'Kitty Peggah'. "Well Meda, we are called 'Street Arabs' because we live on the streets of New York. Those ladies who came with the Bibles gathered a bunch of us, including you and me, to go to a Parish to get a hot meal and discuss a new life. The hot meal was the best part. When we got there, they said because we are destitute, abandoned and have no parents or at least parents who take care of us, and we have been chosen to take the Orphan Train from New York to somewhere on a farm in the middle of the country to a new life."

Meda asked, "What's destitute mean, Charlie?" He replied, "No money I gather. But it ain't right what they say about living on the street and that our mama is a drunk and never got around to getting married so all eleven of us kids could have a father." Meda said, "Well you know, she gets paid for us if we go on The Orphan Train. I think she's glad to get rid of us. But we ain't exactly homeless."

"Don't worry about it Meda. They caught me smokin' a cigarette that my friend, Ole' Smokey gave me. That old bag of a church lady said I was a delinquent, a troublemaker, and should go on a train ride to be 'saved'."

Meda put 'Kitty Peggah' down and he trotted alongside hoping to see his two friends in hopes, they, too, might be going on The Orphan Train.

Meda began to cry. "Do you think I won't get a new dress?" Charlie took hold of her hand and said, "We are going, but I am worried about the twins. What's to come of them? Especially if they get none of the money given for our passage on The Orphan Train. We have been scraping up enough money for leftover bread by selling rags to the paper factory and other food by sweeping Josefe's sidewalk. It's hardly enough just to keep them alive."

"Oh my, let's go. We have to be at the train depot to get checked in and get issued our clothes." Meda looked down at 'Kitty Peggah', "Don't worry. We will figure out how you can be an orphan too."

Later that day, 'Kitty Peggah' went to the Big Iron Horse #384 and said, "With 200 orphans, who is gonna notice if they bring their only possession like me, for instance. Can I jump up in the orphan car? I promise I will stay out of sight and be no trouble." Big Iron Horse #384 said, "Go for it. I know these little people are really scared. It might help calm them down."

"You look real nice, Meda. Don't think I have ever seen your hair combed before, much less a new dress and a bow," Meda giggled. "You're funny, Charlie. You look real good, too."

"Get ready. They are going to load us up soon. Where's 'Kitty Peggah'?" Meda smiled and said, "Don't ask."

"Charlie, do you think Mama will miss us and be sorry we are gone?" What are kind, Christian homes?" asked Meda. "How would I know. Quit asking so many questions. I imagine that means they are good, and we'll have to start going to church! Now, try and get some sleep."

The big Iron Horse #384 with 'Kitty Peggah', the self-appointed engineer, traveled across the vast land that looked nothing like New York City. The abandoned and homeless children were delivered to waiting farmers and others who were anxiously waiting in old warehouse buildings to 'pick' their child. 'Kitty Peggah' said, "Iron Horse #384, are they going to display them like chickens at the market? Charlie will not let Meda go to anyone unless he is with her. He will run away with us in tow. I better run and catch up. Don't want to be lost in the crowd. Much obliged Iron Horse #384. Good job!"

"Meda, stay close with 'Kitty Peggah'. If they start selling us off like those black slaves in the South, we are bailin' outa here."

"Henry, Henry, look at that little girl with the oversized bow. Is that her brother? What's your name? "Meda, and that's my brother, Charlie, and this is 'Kitty Peggah' and we came ...." "Be still, Meda," cautioned Charlie.

"Well, we are Henry and Martha Winser and we have a big farm five miles from here. Does your cat like milk? "I don't know. Doubt he's ever had any," grinned Meda. Martha Winser took Meda's hand and Henry asked Charlie if he was hungry because Martha had fixed a picnic basket. "Meda asked Charlie "What is a picnic basket?" "Shh, Meda. I'm thinkin' it's a good thing. It must have been that new dress and hair bow that did it. Looks like we won't be going back to the streets of New York," smiled Charlie. Kitty Peggah crawled up beside Meda in the wagon not too far from the picnic basket. "Not sure what's in there, but it sure smells good. And what is this about milk?"

Between 1854 - 1929

The Iron Horse transported and relocated 250,000 orphan children from crowded coastal cities to the country's Midwest for fostering and adoption.

Chapter Seven
The Depot #33 Station That Cried

The fog was thick, and a morning chill that went all the way to the bone. Typical winter day in 1861. The Depot Station #33 was reflecting this morning back to the good old days and said out loud. "'Kitty Keragous', do you remember when the Madison and Indianapolis Railroad prospered during the time of the little engine, Elkhorn? How its coach and hog-carrying box cars only traveled eight miles per hour up that unbelievable incline? No one would believe that the cars were let down 413 feet by gravity after which they were hauled back by eight horses."

"Amazing indeed, but just a memory now," said 'Kitty Keragous'.

"Speaking of memories, what a day it was in 1847 when the railroad was completed. Eeryone was in a celebration mood. All 86 miles from Madison to Indianapolis." 'Kitty Keragou's said, "The noise was so loud coming from the enthusiastic crowd waiting on that shrill whistle of the locomotive to come huffing and puffing down the track. They cheered when they saw the long line of passenger and freight cars."

"Don't forget my fresh coat of paint inside and out," said Depot Station #33. Why I was the best-looking depot for miles around."

"Well, it only took 25 years for them come out of the woods!" laughed 'Kitty Keragous'.

The Depot Station #33 looking sad, said, "So much has happened. The incline didn't work out. The State made a decision to make a new route because the old incline had too many operational issues. Even the 'Brough's Folley' ended up a bust. Why I hear people talking about families leaving and it does feel like the town is growing quieter. I so miss the hustle and bustle the trains brought as they rolled through town."

'Kitty Keragous' said, "Now, all people talk about is the Civil War and how long it will last. Some say it could last until 1865 or more."

Depot Station #33 said, "You are so right. In fact, the train that is now called Jefferson Railroad just left this morning carrying a 'precious cargo' of young voices. Why, they don't look old enough to even shave. Singing, smoking, telling stories and full of patriotism. The little regiment was given a loud send off with torch lights, drums, and fanfare ... now fading behind them. I submit, they soon will be sleeping after the long day they have had. Just youngsters being lulled by the shaking of the train to the next depot. Many of the boys looked back as the train pulled away from the station, waving to the sea of handkerchiefs from many mothers, fathers, and girlfriends saying goodbye."

'Kitty Keragous' remarked, "Many parents are thinking about now that their homes were just emptied of noisy, robust boys who may never return ... at least not as children." "We can only hope that the clock that has started ticking will take them through winter, spring, summer, and the beautiful fall, and they will return by next Christmas."

"Let's hope that includes each and every one of them," said the sentimental old Depot Station #33, wiping a tear.

Chapter Eight
When You are Drinking the Water, Remember Who Dug the Well

Wang Lei, a plucky youngster, leaned against the cooler, shaded wall at the Brown's Station Camp waiting on the early morning crew to begin another twelve-hour day. The sixth day this week. Several sleepy-eyed young men seen earlier gulping rice and tea came running across the Nevada desert to catch up. Each had the same dream — come to America. Be free. Be rich.

'Kitty Karakadak', a golden colored cat with one black eye, asked his old friend, The Brown's Station Camp, "Where did all these little, funny-looking people who talk even funnier come from?" He replied, "Oh, they are what's called free immigrants from China. They are here to build the First Transcontinental Railroad. 'Kitty K', affectionately called by his friend, asked "Why do they call them Coolies?" The Brown's Station Camp replied, "Workers who will work long hours without complaint, and low wages is my best guess. I know one thing, they are racing to get ahead of the weather. They are the crew who will remove the soil and rock that keeps the grade at a steady level for the coming railway. Kitty K told The Brown's Station Camp he was off to meet his friend, Gengi, who was a golden color like him only with no black ear, and Nuan, the happiest little feline around. They will be traveling now with the Chinese workers who move with the railroad.

Each day 'Kitty K', 'Genji', and 'Nuan' run alongside the Chinese workers. Everyone knows how important all their jobs are because building the First Transcontinental Railroad will be history making. The Central Pacific Railroad is to connect from the West to the Union Pacific Railroad from the East. All 1085 miles. Without the nearly 11,000 men working in backbreaking conditions, the race to lay the last rail would not have happened.

But, on May 10, 1869, in Promontory, Utah, they did it!! The Golden Spike was struck! The East coast was connected to the West coast. 'Kitty K', 'Genji', and 'Nuan' had completed the journey just like the Chinese workers moving with the railroad. Each hoping to reach their dream destination.

Weng Lei, his father, and brother survived. They opened a Chinese laundry. No more hot days walking many miles with little food and sleep. Now everyone sleeps near the hot tubs of water listening for the little bell to ring telling them that someone is picking up their laundry. In free America, dreams do happen.

Nearly 15,000 Chinese Americans lived and died making the First Continental Railroad a reality.

Many Chinese workers who crossed the Pacific Ocean in search of a better life by making railroad history have been forgotten.

Chapter Nine
Papa, Please Let Me Go with You Today.
They're Opening the New Depot!

'Kitty Kravens' said, "I'm too excited to breathe, huffed the old, roughly put together shack that has been the Depot #77 for more years than some can remember."

"I'm getting a new face lift. A new frame they call it with insulated boards and paint! Why sometimes, it's cold enough in here you could hang meat."

'Kitty Kravens' ran in and out listening to all the celebration noises. A sign was going up called "The Whitewater Valley Railroad Depot." Wow! Now, that will put us on the map, he yelled."

The new look Depot #77 commented, "We are called The WVR DEPOT for short now. They've changed our name a few times. Because our train runs along the Towpath of the Whitewater Canal, we were once called White Water Valley Canal Railroad. However, our canal cannot seem to ever make up its mind between flooding all the time or drought. So, we got new owners and a new name again."

"I don't 'Kitty Kravens'. All I know is its opened now to anyone who wants to ride the short line the 76 miles to Lawrenceburg. Why we can have room for people to either board or be a destination and be greeted by friends and family."

"I see Farmer Lloyd Larsen and his son Lars out here enjoying the celebration. He and other farmers on their horse-drawn wagons bring their goods here while others now send all kinds of things to us. This helps keep our community runnin' and without us the train would just keep on goin'," said the very excited WVR Depot.

"Hi Lars!" 'Kitty Kravens' ran to see his friend who dreams of becoming a train conductor. Lars could not wait for the train to stop. Conductor, Robert Fairhouse came down to the celebration and thanked everyone for making such a welcoming "Depot" for all to enjoy. He said he knows, like other depots, it would be a gathering place for people to meet, socialize, and hear the latest news. Lars ran as fast as he could because Conductor Fairhouse told him the next time he came, he would let Lars see his pocket watch. "Mr. Fairhouse, Conductor Fairhouse, it's me, Lars! Would you show me and Kitty Kravens your pocket watch with the big numbers, please?" I wanna be a conductor when I grow up so I can get a pocket watch just like yours."

"Lars," Conductor Fairhouse said, "we have to be quick because I have to get back to the train. My watch tells me we must be moving on soon. It is so nice to see there will be a ticket office, a waiting room and even separate building for freight business. This is exciting for sure! I tell you what. Let's ask your father if you and your friend Kitty Kravens could ride the train to Lawrenceburg and back. Then you can see what a Conductor does. It's a lot more that wearing a fine pocket watch."

It seemed like the sun shined a long time that day. As the train left the station, the new WVR Depot, 'Kitty Kravens', and Lars wished the special day would never have to end. Oh! Farmer Lloyd Larsen gave permission for Lars to ride the train — with one stipulation — that he go along as chaperone. Conductor Fairhouse was seen shaking Farmer Larsen's hand and Lars, along with his friend, 'Kitty Kravens' grinning from ear to ear! Lars could not wait to tell his friend, The WVR Depot, all about the turnaround trip to Lawrenceburg. And, that he was already planning for the day that he, too, would wear a Railroad Conductor hat and have his own Railroad Watch.

Depot # 77 said, "I know you will be a good

Conductor, Lars, and I'll be here to greet you every day!"

42

Chapter Ten
Safety - The Forgotten Component of Railroading

"Wow, Miss Madison is bringing the whole 6th grade class to the Boston & Maine Railroad Stop here at The Andover Station!" 'Kitty Kooney' bellowed.

"Just what we need," said 'The Andover Station.' A bunch of eleven-year-olds screamin' and runnin' all over the place! Not just to see the President-elect, Franklin Pierce, the 14th U.S. President to be elected; but to see his eleven-year-old son, Benny (Benjamin)!"

'Kitty Kooney' said, "But who gets to get up close and see a new President and his family two months before the inauguration? It's history!! Better yet, when the son, is a classroom idle."

The soon-to-be first family are on their way home to pack up for their new home in Washington. "A real treat," said 'Kitty Kooney', the ever positive, look-a-like to a chubby black-gray long tailed racoon.

"Here it comes right on time. The 1:15 Northbound

train heading toward Concord, New Hampshire. Actually, it is just a slow down so President-elect Pierce, his wife, Jane, and their only child, Benny could stand briefly on the deck of the two-car locomotive, and wave at the cheering crowd to include a screaming sixth grade class."

Benny is smiling ear to ear and waving to his fan Club. 'Kitty Kooney' giggled.

The quaint, old, and simple passenger station greeted the entire field trip class on a very cold January day. They were all dressed in warm hats, scarves, and mittens and waving homemade flags. They were celebrating a day to remember ... in more ways than one.

"Help! Help! There's been a train wreck. A car hit some rocks on the track and they think an axle may have broken," screamed a man, covered with blood, running down the track. The train cars derailed, and they toppled off the embankment and plunged about twenty-five feet below."

"That's awful," said The Andover Station. Someone just last week said the axles needed to be checked on those trains. "A bit late," frowned 'Kitty Kooney'.

Sadly, the sixth grade class was allowed out of school to attend their idle, Benjamin Pierce, the eleven year old son of President-elect and Mrs. Jane Pierce, funeral service. He was the only casualty of the train crash.

In the weeks following, there was a public outcry for some sort of government action to improve safety on railroads. Letters to Washington told of trains colliding, boilers rupturing, open drawbridges that no one had checked the signals, bridges collapsing under the weight of the new, heavier trains.

The little passenger station quietly remarked, "It's commonly believed safety often takes a back seat to profit and expansion!" 'Kitty Kooney' said, "And no one talks about overworked engineers who suffer from sleep impairment."

Over 200,000 hurt in one year prompted several concerned professionals in the railroad industry to take a long look at safety regulations or lack of.

Pioneers and promotors of the Safety Cause like Edward F. Schneider, a GM of the Cleveland Southwestern & Columbus Railway worked to educate and inspire railroad employees so they would make safety their first consideration at all times. Most important would be to eliminate all accidents. 'Kitty Kooney' said, "I like him and others like him. I heard his speech where he told each employee they should be proud to be labeled "Claims Preventor" not Claims Adjustor or Claims Attorney." He said, "It's up to us, all of us. All accidents are avoidable."

'Kitty Kooney' looked at his friend, The Andover Station and said, "Starting next week, there will be a new sign in front of the Andover Station' in large letters for all to see. The sign is: WE PRACTICE FOR A SAFE AND SANE EVERYDAY."

The Andover Station said, "You'd make a good Safety Engineer,' Kitty Kooney'."

Chapter Eleven
You Gonna Rob a Train That's Runnin' Down the Track? Not Good!!

It's October and the leaves have started to turn crimson red, orange, and yellow with a spattering of green still waiting on the next frost. "It's about time for the annual auction of unopened, unclaimed packages, suitcases or anything left on the Wells Fargo stagecoaches to be held," reminded the Indiana Central Railroad Depot #7. 'Kitty Scarlet' asked, "Is it still to the highest bidder?" "Yup, and the conductor on the train going from Cincinnati to Chicago says there are quite a few bidders coming in on the train including a lady from the East being one of them," said Depot #7.

"Why you suppose that?" asked 'Kitty Scarlet'. "I can't imagine anything in all that dusty stuff any lady would want." "Story goes," Depot #7 said, "Her daddy was killed by one of those stagecoach robbers and she thinks his suitcase of personal things might be here." "Oh! Those robbers seem to be everywhere these days. They've been robbing banks, looting, and setting businesses on fire. They even rob people just sitting on a train that has stopped at a depot," 'Kitty Scarlet' said with a scowl.

Depot #7 said, "I used to be afraid of the James Gang and the Younger Brothers. They tore up everything in sight and stole everything that was not nailed down including the safe. If they couldn't open it, they just took it to the desert and dynamited it open. But, let me tell you, those Reno Brothers are worse than any of those hooligans crawling the earth."

'Kitty Scarlet' leaned over, scratched behind her ear, and whispered, "Did you know those Reno Brothers made money by enlisting in the Union Army? Not for patriotism nor duty but for profit. Because a man would pay a bounty for another to fight in his place, they became 'bounty jumpers' then they just kept the money." "Their mama didn't whoop them hard enough, I'm thinkin'," said Depot #7. Those boys ain't been right since their daddy ran off to be with one of those vigilante groups and got himself killed in the crossfire."

"Wait, wait. The last thing I heard coming across the telegraph wire is two of the Reno Brothers gang just held up an Ohio & Mississippi train — a moving train! They went into the Adams Express Company car, beat up the guard and took $10,000 in gold coins by throwing the safe out the side door. Two more brothers were waiting to blow the door off the safe and run. Kitty Scarlet shivered and said, "I'm getting really nervous that our train could be next; but right now we need to go off and see who gets off the train for the auction. Frankly, I would love a nap first."

Pinkerton Detectives, some unknown men all dressed in black, the regular Wells Fargo attendees of the past, and a beautiful, tiny, very fancy dressed lady with a feathered hat all exited when the train came to a full stop and the Conductor pulled down the steps.

"Let's get started," said Depot #7. Bring out the first package, Mr. Auctioneer. The bids went at a normal pace with most of the seasonal buyers participating. The auctioneer shouted, "#8 Suitcase. No padlock, no name." Immediately, the little lady said, "$10." The audience all looked at one another and the Auctioneer said, "That's a pretty high bid for a suitcase." The lady spoke up in a soft voice and said, "My father was killed by some robbers on the stagecoach and his personal things are in there." All bidding on the suitcase stopped and the Auctioneer said, "Sold to the little lady with the green feathered hat." She quickly paid the $10, took the suitcase and headed back to the train.

Just as she started to board, Pinkerton Detectives walked up alongside her, took a hold of her arm and said, "Mrs. Mayberry, that is your name isn't it?" Please come with us, you are under arrest!" Detective Butler said, "Open the suitcase." She jerked her arm away and said, "Well, I never," and got a handkerchief and started dabbing her eyes.

Pinkerton officer said, "We have been investigating the Wells Fargo stagecoach robbery where a stolen shipment of bank money was being transported, and a Wells Fargo Agent was killed. A snitch told us that it was planned that an unmarked, locked suitcase would eventually make its way to Depot #7 and held for claim or sold at the annual auction with all the other unclaimed packages that were safely held in storage.

Pinkerton Detectives expected one of the Reno Gang to appear as one of the businessmen who regularly attend auctions. They usually bought and sold many packages and made a very lucrative living doing it. The snitch told them sometimes they sent a lady of the gang. The net had been cast. "Patience and perseverance will usually pay off," said the Pinkerton Detective in charge. He sternly said, "Your name is not Melda Maybery but Marna Reno, wife of notorious bank robber and killer, Simeon Reno. He is wanted in several states for theft and murder." "Handcuff her and shoot the lock off."

Seeing all that bank money that had been sitting in the storeroom was a jaw dropping experience for 'Kitty Scarlet', Depot #7, and the entire audience watching the auction. "Boy this is like no other," a regular participant commented.

"Boy, oh boy, we have had enough excitement for one day 'Kitty Scarlet' sighed in relief. All of a sudden, the three men in black with scarlet covered neckerchiefs around their necks did not get back on the train. "Who are they?" Depot #7 asked the Auctioneer. "Well, you won't hear much, or see much written about them. In time, you will know a lot about them. They are the members of the 'Scarlet Mask Society'. I am an undercover Pinkerton Detective. We work well with this organized band of vigilantes who have been following the notorious Reno Gang brothers, their members, and other notorious robbers, thieves and killers of innocent people."

Their unpublished motto:

Shoot first and ask questions later and immediate lynching at the nearest tree upon capture.

Already, pieces of rope or bark from the hangin' tree are becoming popular souvenirs.

It is believed that by taking the law in their own hands without publicity of their whereabouts, they can quietly and effectively rid many small communities of these menacing gangs.

A Year Later

'Kitty Scarlet' with her scarlet-colored bandana lay basking in the sun of Depot #7's new porch on a beautiful mahogany bench. Three, well dressed men arrived on a freight train with no billing. "Another question you don't ask," said Depot #7 grinning at 'Kitty Scarlet'.

Less and less train robberies, bank holdups, and killings were reported in the area, and no arrests were ever made of the "Scarlet Mask Society" members. As part of the Pinkerton Agencies report, no names were ever used.

"Why do we know this?" Because 'Kitty Scarlet' and Depot #7, the honorary members of the "Scarlet Mask Society" told us so.

Chapter Twelve
Build a Railroad to The Yukon River!
What a Joke! How Foolish Is That!

'Kitty Buffy' didn't particularly like the way the "Old Yukoner," who he had traveled many years with to all the passes to the Yukon River — coast to coast, was talking. "What's all this nonsense about gold and the future route for gold fields ,'Kitty Buffy' asked.

"Well, for a lynx with fur as thick as a fur winter coat and someone with absolutely no social skills, you sure are talkative all of a sudden. What happened to my 'ghost cat?'"

'Kitty Buffy', there is a railway called The Tahu-Teslin Railway (Yukon short Line) that The Yukon Mining, Trading and Transportation Company says has been perfected for a railway from the Pacific Coast to the navigable waters of the Yukon," said the Old Yukoner. "What in the world for?" said the very curious, gray lynx.

"Gold! My little fur buddy. I have always said more money can be made from supplying things to the miners then in actual mining. You know, carrying miners to and from their mines. Supply them with food, tools, clothing and machinery."

'Kitty Buffy' lowered his head and said, "But what about me? You know the Missus will have her litter and many others as well in late summer and early fall. Mrs. Buffy immediately starts teaching them hunting skills on how to survive. But, you know from our travels during a gold rush, those miner crazies will kill about anything in sight. They don't care if the little guys do or don't have survival skill training. Those guys are just mean for the sake of meanness. They could wipe out the snowshoe hare as well as the Dall sheep populations in one season and that does not even talk about the lynx families. They don't even eat us, just kill for the fun of it. Get them drinkin' that homemade stuff, they just go on a shooting rampage, and none is for food survival.

The Old Yukoner ran his hand through the long tufts on his faithful friend's ears and the tip of his black tipped tail. With compassion, he said, "The idea of building a railroad from the Pacific Coast to the Yukon River and call it the Alaskan-Yukon Arctic Railroad was a joke and termed just plain foolishness. But all of a sudden, it made sense. You are almost twelve years old, and I lost count of my age, except we do know that I'm gettin' up in age. People won't believe we traveled the 450 miles of Yukon flats many times, but we know those days are getting few and far between."

'Kitty Buffy' scooted up along his friend and listened. "You hear all these expeditions being planned. It is just a matter of time until they will find what we already know. Gold and more gold in these rivers. We need to settle ourselves into a business as provider of goods and services ahead of the railway. An easier way to make a living wouldn't you say?"

'Kitty Buffy' rubbed the leg of his oldest and best friend. "Maybe a new Train Depot and General Store might look pretty good. Besides that, I'm gettin' too old for all those kittens hangin' around!"

"So, said the Old Yukoner, we still partners?"

'Kitty Buffy' grinned. "Yup and we know where the gold is ... we just ain't ever tellin'. Let's go do a little gold pannin' before the river gets too high. Think we better do a little planning for the future."

Chapter Thirteen

Is There Time for Apple Pie? The Long Sliding Stop - Tangiers

It's a cloudless day near Rush Creek. The Brazil Division of the Chicago and Eastern Illinois Railroad surveyors are busy with plotting out what will be a railroad track running through the Valley along Rush Creek.

'Kitty Yedo', the resident, newly self-appointed post office #14 Postmaster Assistant remarked, "Our little community is getting a name! I heard Captain T.J. Campbell is going to name us Tangier, and it will be plated by the end of the month. 'Kitty Yedo' said, "Tangier? Africa? Hot?" "Yup, but most will call it 'The Long Sliding Stop' 'cause the next stop is a mile East. You could just slide the train there! Because Captain Campbell fought in Morocco, Africa, he decided the area reminded him of Tangier."

The Post Office #14 decided it was a pretty nice name. "You know, many settlers have come here at one time or another because their wagons broke down or family members had to be buried due to the measles epidemic. Many families could not see leaving their children alone buried in a strange place."

"The Yoders settled here but bet you don't know why," said 'Kitty Yedo'. "Okay. Tell me," Post Office #14 said.

"Well, when they were coming across the Valley near Rush Creek, Mr. Harlin Yoder saw a big, what appeared to be, an orchard of apples. He stopped so everyone could run up the hill and pick a few. They were beautifully ripened. He climbed one of the trees and shook the apples into Mrs. Yoder and the two girls' aprons. The tree was so full and there were apples all over the ground. Mr. Yoder got down from the tree and to the Yoder family said, "This is a gift from above and we aren't going any farther."

"Wow, now that is a story for the history books," Post office #14 said with a huge smile.

'Kitty Yedo' continued. "And, when the Railroad was built, the Yoders helped build the covered bridge and the land they settled on was rich in coal. Later, the Indiana Coal Railroad ran across their land. Mrs. Yoder attended every community meeting to make sure no one cut or damaged any tree in the apple orchard. But many railroad men and those who helped build the railroad, shared in some fresh apple pie from time to time, and the Yoder Roadside Stand is a thriving business with pies, jams, jellies and Apple Betty, a Yoder specialty."

"Do you think they have apples in Africa?" giggled 'Kitty Yedo'. Post Office #14 shook his head. "Now where did that came from?"

Chapter Fourteen
A Ghost of a Ride

George, the L&N Railroad Conductor with his starched looking dark, navy coat with freshly polished gold buttons and official cap, turned his head curiously to listen for the clicking of the telegraph signaling the arrival of the next train.

"Good morning Conductor George," said 'Kitty Knittyspin' playfully chiding his old friend. "She could sure find your hopes, couldn't she?" As they walked to the L&N Train Depot, it was the slender, blue-eyed girl gracefully walking out of the L&N Depot that caught his eye.

The L&N Depot said "Okay, you two put your eyes back in your head. She is the new owner of the Brunsy Hotel and Spindletop Mercantile. Her parents were lost in that horrific train wreck when the train jumped the track in that ice storm."

Conductor George, who has been concerned over safety of his trains said, "I think that one is still under investigation since everyone knows it could have been avoided."

"Just so you know, Miss Brunsy lets me lay on her front porch," grinned 'Kitty Knittyspin'. "I get to watch her spin all sorts of wool on that Saxony wheel, she calls it. She walks around the spindle checking the pattern and sings hymns. Sometimes when the big wheel is getting louder, oh my goodness, that thing comes roaring back like a big bear coming out of the woods."

"George, I gotta tell you guys something else," whispered 'Kitty Knittyspin'. "Okay, spit it out, I still have to get on the incoming train and get to Crescent Hill." The L&N Depot spoke up." I gotta telegraph to listen to."

"Well," said 'Kitty Knittyspin', "she has a ghostly air about her and an obsession with cleanliness. She wears out brooms from sweeping and dusting rags. She told me she abhorred dirt and her hotel would always be clean enough for even a ghost to live. Even right down to the chimney. Do you think she is a ghost?" The conductor walked toward his train now noisily blasting its' entrance coming down the track, looked back and said, "Well, if she is a ghost, she is a comely one."

A hectic hustle and bustle morning with Conductor George attending to all who departed. He glanced at the stately house across the street with its new sign "BRUNSEY

HOTEL AND SPINDLETOP MERCANTILE" and there she was sweeping off the wrap around porch. The walnut rockers with neatly arranged homemade pillows were obviously some of her handiworks from her spinning wheel. She was a welcome sight. 'Kitty Knittyspin' yelled, "Hey Conductor George. Come on over, we are now open for business. Get your room before we fill up."

Conductor George made The Brunsey Hotel and Spindletop Mercantile his residence between train runs, and eventually got up the nerve to ask Miss Brunsey to attend Sunday church escorted by 'Kitty Knittyspin', of course.

As the years passed, the love between Conductor George and Miss Brunsey flourished. It wasn't until the traveling trains and patrons of the hotel came from areas where water was unknowingly contaminated that things began to change. The L&N Train Depot and 'Kitty Knittyspin' started hearing rumors of a typhoid fever epidemic. "I'm worried," said 'Kitty Knittyspin' to his friends. "Miss Brunsey called Dr. Hutchings from Park City to come look at a little eight-year-old girl who came down with a high fever last night. They fear all the hotel guests might be exposed to typhoid fever.

The L&N Train Depot just got a telegraph. "All

trains cancelled until all trains with passengers who are showing symptoms of typhoid fever have been administered to!!" Conductor George was so relieved to see Dr. Hutchings had arrived.

Conductor George, Miss Brunsey, 'Kitty Knittyspin', and Dr. Hutchings sat with the parents of little Lizzy whose frail little body did not make it through the night. Typhoid fever is rampant.

Miss Brunsey has been scrubbing everything in sight. Dr. Hutchings reminded all of them. "It is a bad fever caused by nothing you did or did not do." The numbers in the hotel of fatalities began to climb. Miss Brunsey began to show signs of getting weaker and weaker until she was put to bed by Dr. Hutchings. 'Kitty Knittyspin' and Conductor George sat vigil and gave reports but none were good.

Miss Brunsey called for Conductor George and 'Kitty Knittyspin' to her bedside. She said "I want you both to know, I must leave you but Lizzy and my spirit will be with you always. We shall appear on occasion so you will know my love will always be yours. Someday you can join us. For now, my darlings, please take care of each other and L&N Railroad Depot."

Life was never the same. It is told, however, that

several years later when Conductor George passed away, he joined Miss Brunsey and was seen passing his "ghostly" time between the Hotel Brunsey and Spindletop Mercantile and the L&N Railroad Depot. Even today, he is known to take great exception if someone moves, touches, or fusses with his dark, navy coat with the shiny buttons. Reports tell how some have felt his admonishment to leave his personal things alone or feel the consequences.

This is reported by the ancestors of 'Kitty Knittyspin, and is of good authority'.

Chapter Fifteen
The Mail Goes — No Matter What, Just Ask Cupie Mast!

His real name is Cephus Ulysis Penrod Ishket Eldon Mast. They call him 'Cupie' Mast for short. "Why do they always name us after dead people or silly names no one can pronounce or spell?" "Well, 'Kitty Aloysius', by your name, you are a famous warrior. At least that's what your name implies," said Phalanax Station. "Look at me. 'Phalanax!' What kind of made-up name is that? I'm thinkin' someone had too much spirits that day. At least we can all say 'Cupie'"

'Cupie' patiently waits on the LEA&W sliding into Hopedale. Once the bag and boxes are laced in his cart, off he goes to the Hopedale Post Office.

"Consarn it! Seems every time them gal-darned first graders get to take a field trip to get an ice cream cone, it becomes the longest twenty-mile return trip of the century," said 'Cupie' Mast. "Don't they know I have important work to be done! Mail to sort and boxes to unbox. Well, I happen to know Miss Florish is waiting on a new bonnet she ordered from the East."

'Kitty Aloysius' walked at the edge of his friend, Phalanax Station and quietly said, "You know Phalanax Station, 'Cupie' Mast is gettin' up in age a bit and some folks say his mind is a bit out of register." "I know, remarked Phalanax Station, but he doesn't get mad when we gently correct him. The other day he came in to the Station and remarked Miss Florish had come in looking for her new hat she had ordered and on her neck was a lockup with a picture in it." I said, "You mean locket, 'Cupie'? "Yup, and it was a beauty just like her."

"Important thing, 'Kitty Aloysius', 'Cupie' knows about mail. Only job he has ever had. I figure it's okay if he talks funny. Like our names, we are all different."

"I agree, and I hear the train slowing down, so I gotta get to the mail cart and help 'Cupie'. See ya later," grinned 'Kitty Aloysius'.

'Cupie' Mast shouted, "Move outa the way, mail cart comin' through." About that time, the town bullies, Wada and Walter Jarvis yelled, "Can we hitch a ride old man?" 'Cupie' Mast looked up and said, "Nope - nothin' rides my cart but the mail and 'Kitty Aloysius' who keeps the mail from falling out and getting lost." Just as the two boys grabbed 'Kitty Aloysius's tail, he flew up, ears got straight as a board, and his back arched so high, it pulled his feet off the ground. What happened next, both 'Cupie Mast and Phalanax Station watched in total shock and later it was reported.

'Kitty Aloysius', the heroic warrior, walked away without a scratch, 'Cupie' Mast had to wipe a little dirt off his Post Office britches, and Miss Florish's new hat arrived safely without a ruffled feather. The town bullies, Wada and Walter ... well no one is talkin'.